TO STIR &

OR
EVEN IF IT HURTS SO MUCH I CAN ONLY FIND
ENOUGH BREATH LEFT TO DANCE

POEMS

# NIKIA CHANEY

SELECTED BY CYNTHIA ARRIEU-KING
FOR THE HILARY THAM CAPITAL COLLECTION

THE WORD WORKS
WASHINGTON, D.C.

*to stir* & © 2023 Nikia Chaney

Reproduction
of any part
of this book
in any form
or by any
means, electronic
or mechanical,
except when
quoted in
part for the
purpose of
review, must
be with
permission
in writing
from the
publisher.
Address
inquiries
to:

THE WORD WORKS
P.O. Box 42164
Washington, D.C. 20015
editor@wordworksbooks.org

Cover art: Janine Aberg, "The Systems Which Drive Our Lives"
Cover design: Susan Pearce

LCCN: 2022947363
ISBN: 978-1-944585-57-0

# Acknowledgments

Thanks to the editors who first published these poems:

*Moira Poetry*: "and another one"

*Journal X*: "think of the beet"

*The Future is Black: Afrofuturism, Black Comics, and Superhero Poetry* (Blair Publishing, 2021): "spinnerman"

*Peregrine XXXV: Black Poets Speak*: "or on tv the astrophysics"

*Porter Gulch Review*: "a plain of rigidity"

*Clockhouse Journal*: "not about the kink"


In my first book I meant to thank so so many people for all that they have brought to me. let me fix this by thanking you all here. any book is, after all, just a culmination of moments learning from others. you have all touched my life in one way or another and I am so honored to know you.

**CC**: thank you Nikki Giovanni, Toi Derricotte, Cornelius Eady, Lyrae Van Clief-Stefanon, Chris Abani, Amber Flora Thomas, Tim Siebles, Willie Perdomo, Terrence Hayes, Nikky Finney, Angela Jackson, Patricia Smith, Alison Meyers, Amanda Johnston, and Tyehimba Jess, for all that you are taught and shared with me; and a I'd like to special shout out to Makalani Bandele, Destiny Birdsong, Malika S Booker, F. Douglas Brown, Mahogany L. Browne, Cortney Lamar Charleston, Tameka Cage Conley, Yolanda J. Franklin, Anya Creightney, Vida Cross, Geffrey Davis, Sean DesVignes, Alyss Dixson, Mary Moore Easter, T'ai Freedom Ford, Aricka Foreman, Ross Gay, Alysia Nicole Harris, Zakia Lorraine Henderson-Brown, Chinaka Hodge, Juliet P. Howard, Ashaki M. Jackson, Gary Jackson, Khary Jackson, Douglas Kearney, Robin Coste Lewis, Steven Leyva, Gary Lilley, Maya A Marshall, Dawn Lundy Martin, Airea Dee Matthews, Nathan McClain, M'Bilia M. Meekers,

Dante Micheaux, Ciara Miller, Tracie Morris, Harryette Mullen, Angel Nafis, Rachel Nelson, Ife-Chudeni A. Oputa, Ladan Osman, Morgan Parker, Kathy Z. Price, Magali Roy-Fequiere, Lauren Russell, Aaron Samuels, Nicole Sealey, Charif Shanahan, Aisha Sharif, Rose Smith, Sasha Warner-Berry, and Maya Washington, for helping me find my tribe.

**csusb**: thank you Juan Delgado, Julie Sophia Paegle, Chad Sweeney, James Brown, Jessica Lewis Luck, Karen Rowan, Ellen M. Gil-Gomez, and Glen Hirshberg, for your attention to my work and of course, Michael Thomas Cooper, Ashley Hayes, Eric Atkinson, Shali Nicholas, Connie Lopez Hood, Elisa Urmston, Casey Goodson, Sara Gerber, Bryan Henery, Nicole Comstock, Joseph A. Huver, Melissa Sonico, Chris Shaw, Marsha Lee Binnquist Schuh, Orlando Ramirez, Angela Thomson Brenchley, Reanna Marchman Smith, Melissa Fowler, Andre Katkov, Tristan Douglas, Chrysta Wong-Sierra, Justin Elgar, and Isaac Escalera for reading poems with me.

**antioch**: thank you Alistair McCartney, Jenny Factor, Carol Potter, Richard Garcia, Ben Doller, Tananarive Due, Xochitl-Julisa Bermejo, Alison Tobey, Lisa McCool-Grime, Gayle Brandeis, Khadija Anderson, Chrys Tobey, Lisa Cheby, Barbara Berg, LaToya Jordan, Armine Iknadossian, Shonda Buchanan, Aya de Leon, Melissa Chadburn, Antonia Crane, Marva Hinton Gibson, Seth Fischer, Tisha Reichle, Tina Ruben, Diane Sherlock for always being there through the years.

**special others**: thank you Patricia S. Jones, Robert Hass, Sharon Olds, Kazim Ali, Cathy Hong, Juan Felipe Herrera, Laurie Posner, Soul Vang, Tristan Silverman, Brett Hall Jones, K.M. English, Cara Murray, Angela Penaredondo, Jamie Goh, Kris Peterson, Tiffany Keeler, Micah Kaguya, Eric "True" DeVaughn, James Coats, Sandra Blackman Flowers, Frances J. Vasquez, Tim Hatch, Laurie Barton, Judy Kronenfeld, Maurisa Thompson, and David Stone.

**uofh press and the word works**: thank you so much for publishing my first book. thank you so much for publishing my second book. thank you so much for what you put out in the world for others.

**santa cruz**: thank you Raina Chelise, Alta Northcutt, Ekua Omosupe, Adela Najarro, Victoria Banales, Geneffa Jonker, and Steve Schessler for being my friend. thank you hive: Danusha Lameris, Dion O'Reilly, Farnaz Fatemi, Julie Murphy, and Julia Chiapella. and thank you David Sullivan, Lisa Sewell, Genevieve Caplan, Anne Kenison, and Elaine Terranova for the attention and insight you always gave to these poems.

**inlandia**: oh how I love you all: Cati Porter, Larry Eby, Maria Douglas Notarangelo, Allyson Jeffrado, Melissa Grant, and Cassidy Parong. thank you E.J. Jones. You all will always be my writing home.

**sisters**: Cynthia Manick, Pamela L. Taylor, Lolita Stewart White, Romaine Washington, Lisa Henry, Ginger Galloway, Amidia Frederick, and for never ever ever ever letting me go.

**babies**: thank you bubba, shushu, billa, yusuf, and riya, for letting me help you grow up.

**you**: and thank you you, dear readers, for listening and dancing just a bit (i imagine you so) with these words.

i love you all!

# Contents

The paper candies the air — 5
***like music like muscle memory***
but does it – swell all jelled — 8
think of the red beet — 10
going to spell — 11
you are spinning — 12
So you — 13
spinnerman — 14
***don't you dare go***
& you keep asking — 16
not about the kink — 17
but her (again) — 18
how do you do it — 19
how they never — 21
decide now — 23
they will insist that — 24
I quit — 25
A plain of rigidity like grass — 27
If I draw you again — 28
***these portraits hanging on sheets***
they look like girl — 30
and another one — 31
a monster — 33
what this — 35
being — 36
her name is what makes — 37
quiero all y — 38
& sometimes I don't even like — 40
***the law & how it makes us***
talk about rockets — 43
so wait — 45
the little girl has won — 47
we are struggling — 52
& everything folds — 53
splay hand open — 55

|  |  |
|---|---|
| & yet again | 58 |
| fight to be this | 60 |
| & if it were under my arm | 61 |
| **joy all hard found & neat** | |
| or on tv | 63 |
| or that is not mean | 64 |
| might even like it | 66 |
| kin's like this | 67 |
| & so we | 68 |
| **sing: drinking muddy water** | |
| black woman be | 73 |
| | |
| About the Author / About the Artist | 83 |
| About The Word Works | 84 |
| The Hilary Tham Capital Collection | 85 |

                              The paper candies the air like
           law while we
    somersault through windows in hallways.
            Our sidewalks looping out in over

                               woven
       runners redlining their geometry
              of stamped

                      lines eyebrows elbows everywhere.
Carpet even unplush and stark
        under the feet.  Really.  And they say we should
                swim. They

           say we can
rise as one right or pester one together
      to augment

ourselves into doubles as if our legs
          were troll and scale.  As if we could
    make the schooling of race and gender

               a pinion fin peeking out above the surface
                  tension a word
                         less wonder or victimless sin. As if we

           could gather all of the diverse
       doctrines into binders which we then close
                        joyfully smiling.
    Defeat with grin. Poising our brown feathers

on one toe while the skewers prick the whites
    of our eyes.

    no, we say
  we ain't that wet. Because of course

   we really all of us are
     are that is learning
      learning always the water taking law the making
  of new ways to fight within the dance of acclimation.

Look. True policy is the law limiting space between us.
  Once there could be community
    or once there was. Or maybe even will be. A togetherness.

     It ain't really so fetch and bold. The disco of norms
     the voice and all the voice.
     Now squawking
  alight like in this here room,

frenetic and full of transit gyred in
      what is real progress: you seeing me as
  I am me seeing you be or should or trying at best to

    spinning up in
   the bowl. Learning to breathe
  and better yet again to stir.

*like music like muscle memory*

                    but does it – swell all jelled together
hurt        the glissando the walk
                through of each pad
                        a thump pressed to string a
hooked graduation of clef plectrum perched
                                on the cliff rise
                            wire a proper type of raging
                            one of survival
                spanning one age to another
trembling in joy
            and always made to be held
            because
            it does
                    hurt and soothe
                    everything
                    the language of            it settling
                                                the past his day
                room a place
where he had to have sat hungry and cut his own
            new muscles into
                shank bracket            mismatched
                                            tattoo scored
dermis even
nagging for cure or     else the half-night
                            of my own husk
                        of childhood that
                            squeal of
neglect its grope
seeping into
small bones      a flayed back my
                    knuckles and patellas on a mat
listening even then
even now           in this

                        moment when this broken man
            whose be is sitting
            on the opposite side of an
unbreakable
screen a whole half-world away    plays me a song
                                            glides from one
                                            pitch to the next
something breaks open in    us solidifies his fingers on
those guitar strings as clear
as a trembling as any composition        as this music
                                            I insist on
                                            talking about
                                            some more
                            that swells and chafes kissing each
                        pinprick horn twang
            resound quake vibrato
            our hard lives
            the pulp of all it cooled
                    the must be
                    glue between

think of the red beet the red like stomachs that turn cartwheels and land splayed on carpets of mud think of the beet the beet's skin the hunger in its depths the need to rub or stretch or scream then think of the beet's voice humming like Norteño the bajo sexto blushed carmine the lime orange ruby lunes and thick strings spread-eagled these your neighbors these children like twangs blinking gold in the water dancing so loud and rowdy we try to wash it not off but in inside our skin brown wet beet skin crinkled and pinched wine red and black brown and think of it the way it slides in the hand heavy the way it walks feet sure and clean knowing how it looks
and how it sounds

going to spell h.o.m.e. like koolaid red and slippery but not
pulsing or heart in palm or the rat tat
of flesh against wall but k o o then sugar so thick
it vibrates your teeth like home like rosé or rosie a thing
my dirt skin can never be because it don't need to be and home
is even wrong four letters the o sound a short horn
that puffs it way past the door to close off the wind when it
should be long an ahh an uh even e slow as the slide of thick
glass to waiting red water splash flittering round the handle and
that's the word right there the knob in knuckles the cold in palm and
the drink hugging and stroking the back of your neck
like fingers so thirsty for touch they only taste you best
wipe off your mouth i want that i got that going on I take that
and write it out in wet     letters across     the porch like an effigy fat
              hereness in my mouth
                      openness in my neck 'cause if i don't then what's

    the use of sweet drinks and holding on what's

            the real reason for    relief that pitcher on the wall

shining open saying thirsty girl you thirsty       yes close the door

       or open it and walk through you belong here

   you arrived     set it down
                    drink it
                              sleep

~~you~~ are <u>spinning</u> a
   water ~~machine~~     drum dress
you <u>caught</u> taunt   round ~~fins~~
mouth a spigot     to <u>catch</u>
<u>water</u>    machine ~~drum~~    dress
   thump pressed     to <u>dance</u> in
<u>mouth</u>      a spigot to ~~catch~~
rain <u>belly</u>      as flat     as
~~thump~~    <u>pressed</u> to dance    in
   to jib on      stamp ~~out~~
<u>rain</u>      belly as ~~flat~~ as
pearl    ~~all~~    <u>lace</u> raveled
~~to~~ jib    <u>on</u>     stamp out
  <u>stillness</u>    ~~this~~ seeping    of
~~pearl~~    all lace    <u>raveled</u>
ready      ~~the~~ circle <u>like</u>
stillness     this    <u>seeping</u> ~~of~~
  ~~you~~      are spinning a
ready the <u>circle</u>     ~~like~~
~~you~~    caught taunt <u>round</u> fins

So you
drive out to Friday streets and busk or rap or dream all about the truth
of prohibition of
ever wanted parole. From the e note acoustic rendition of being
small and needed by some
body stoked by
some large
separate
body
that comes forward this time to a stage to light you open. Your eyes like
a clink a change and ovation of
oval pink lights
that may
just be string stringed. But so what you don't want this body pulling milk from your tits
or crying wasted wailing tears
at the
unfairness
of your life. Your song
rerendered & broke of every blue note so much so
that the yearn to love is just yearn (they all say) for every little
thing. And what
is this
demon of
interpretation anyway where
we really know that we sell our souls every day hoping for the *please* in the
understroke & rhythm
the brimstone
home.

spinnerman brotherman spinnerman needs no intro cause he don't care see his fro but don't touch his hair to him life is spitting a rhyme whenever there is some time you'll find the spiderman in the silence of the night like a shadow from the sky he flies down from his flight cool ass negro oh so fly spinnerman spinnerman makes his body the entire band he can rap upside down take a look he's got a crown hey there there goes the spinnerman watch out here comes the spinnerman where's the drum it's his hand he can roasts the crowd cracks up the room catches rhythms on the ground scratches whatever thing spinnerman spinnerman *don't you dare go*

& you keep asking them   to look
         at you to call you first by each number then by
your name                   a foreign word to sizzle and make

the room     swallow the tv with buzz    cuts and bellies a swell to middle age to clos
         both their eye and yours

but it is getting too late     to pair up    to be couple mama daddy's big piece of chick
plate & holding   it                   down in bed all

scarfs swaddled and snore       they     of course as they would be by the fan where y
& they and they              would

you might              reel    to euphony and breath &
each day's discontent

         too bright    the tv the chuck of it    the sweats the sounds swinging as lo
as the gray
pillow

you don't belong           in these years one twisting arm to ten
& screen blind you keep asking         them to
                     say you are     enough      this         hushful
this has to           this half     to       haves       this way of

| | | | | | |
|---|---|---|---|---|---|
| not about the kink | my scalp or | the plumpness of | this lady | flesh or uterine | to walls of blood |
| or even about momness | baby girls at | the nipple and how I | just wanted | a little bit of everything | and certainty |
| and nothing do with my men | my waist | don't want to talk about | these cubed things | sit in your box | woman and rattle |
| no I'm going to speak | about ready to give | the cold | bright shaft of light | screech through | the expectation of worth |
| less of foolish | toddler pride | which returns babbles | gender lessness | whole means of fruit | or pearl with plate |
| gold and more of brine | good surface relief | glass sorting each wave | each incident to explain | or save me | like my exhale wasn't enough |
| this ain't simple | saving breath | giving out womanness | and posture | like you are listening | like I now must again not speak |

but her – (again) tell her that she has no arms – no want – rather her ripples of math unfold rapidly to cover the clear confidence of her impossibility – there ain't a weaning here – nor loss

of appetite – unzip her ribs and step over each one of her clay steins – scuffle with the patches

of her struggling – her small defeats – the reach around she leaves hanging on the bed to flutter with the added finespun to her levees - the unmade sheet - the post about cornrows and blankets – her nails just long enough to curve round the knots and margins to pretend that

this façade is not wanting her back – make her thirsty - make her braided fancy – recite to her

the news of the revolution humming so glitzy in the want of it you both start to swoon – sing it then and feed her arms and candy to untwist each strand of her with your whole body like you really are a silhouette of shea butter and she cannot sprout alone just lying there – make

her add up – one piece slowly unraveled to one flash via the sob and shake (i.e.) the cushions on

the couch under her spine – she is joining in slowly she is smiley and queued, a being of touch plaited – come – come you – come here you – and define wage war – calculate her – then knock her down – the breastbone like so much silky dust caught in the room's quiet breeze – the relief

how do you     do it shake the hand of the muse
ask the god of it     to come down sip wine on the porch

what if you don't     drink wine
or have     a porch or couldn't make it

yesterday because the getting     up out of bed was too hard what
if you didn't     sleep and all the want of it

laid out on your     tomorrow is blinking a mouth
hungry in the ear     its own ocean like a culling

of your own breath     whatever you are whatever is
up there know I have a question     damnit I am walking on

sheet metal I am opening     doors and I want to know the worth

of these teeth     that unfurl like
the ugly parts of balloons     jagged as these pages

of keys for there is     steel in the gristle
you formed or I     formed like charting wordsmith

skin in tall     glasses of diction yogalike on both
our cheeks that make us scar how     the hell do we capture that

or remember learning to speak to touch     you calm
treachery     me silent a needling

snipping the lingual frenulum to sand     down thin
ankle bones     so I can still stroll

with the memory of limping          so you can
hush royally with all          this pain haven't I asked for you

to handle me          and the gentle shame
enough  & haven't we done this already before

how they
never
tell you
when they sit
you down
to draw red
head bands on
forehead and paint
fingers with mud
your feet in
scented pools
ready for the banquet
or the feast
that the war
might mean
martyrdom
you bride or you
conscript
may need to expose
neck belly sex
to the enemy
to the jealousy
to the inability
of the small death
to hold any
one palpable
object that can be
left unrotten
and bling you may
fall not in
arms or armed
but with bundles
of kindling open

flexed your own
breath a spark
and worse
wedded to self
sacrificed to dowry
fatigues
all downy silks
like knives on
sheath no armor
or reward for
if you
knew it love
as suicide
as inverted
anger as body
piercing body
you might run
full force
into fields lose
a leg to mine
that first kiss
laying you up
all broke
in the grunt
and trench
of someone
anyone's
arms.

*after Yehuda Amichai "ballad on the streets of buenos aires"*

Decide now	choose for if I	were that being	that other being that
meets brown	that wants	as the beetle inching its slow
way to eat	eat that	that other being that sees and stops to pause

to lift up	slowly off the ground	as if there were	were violins
that hum	that their wood	that stretch past us	us learning to touch to
gather to spread	this this thing that	we that find in our	stumbling way together

the dirt on the back	the back of the chatter	of legs on the other's wrists
tickling like a neck is	is being exposed the light	light changing from
dark to	red to	yellow to	a whole sphere	going backwards this	this lifting

this tying the strings of us to	to ground the beneath and I am	I am afraid held
so high	so in this	so of this other	this other's body	perhaps we would decide to
to let it go	to fall apart	to dive back down	to that that one	that that enough

                                                they will insist that
                    inmost is the frantic motion. but clap
                             back and regard
                 the unreality of the closed body
            verbing as something more
              authentic than the desire
                             to change positions. be at bay
in the shell. hate it (just
          a bit) but listen
               for the bells to ring to
scream time to
                 go out and visit again. cram
          your rind into each other. lift mask to
                              kiss where
                by the room emerges
    a strange smell. the pores are leaking. the saliva
                  swerving to bare
    again the bones. there are baskets of baked goods
                      for this. mirrors
that choose not to
                 reflect to
                    help you. genial flowers on
         the path
                 wave by
                         the open door. colorblind
those flowers are that coming
            smell of breath. waiting nurdled
                         for that's you now
                       looking at
                me now
                        out
      side dancing nudged.

I quit two days ago and tried running from the world
took book and con cornrow and pen

and tried to flap my brownness into feathers

or sneakers or suction cups money
it seems both tasting bad and tasting good
a means to be a sort of free where i

could feed my own children on giggles
and the dream of time like i wasn't branded in some

public housing project (work) or academic pursuit (think) but
then the phone rang another humanity

lesson needed another matriculation another lost

white (or hey black) child closed eyed enough
to sit privileged-like in my chair and ask
or not ask where i been home

less or where i been crazy house or what it is

poverty which ain't colorful ain't easily seen and I
guess in the trying to tell (clean) I forgot about the way it slants

the horizon as you move towards it the sound

of silence the only bridge to sit between
the wheels running in the soles of my leg
and the slimness of enough after all I made

it right I got us out and doesn't it feel so good this
stark clean life halls and offices lined

up like teeth two
days ago i almost made it I almost got out

messed it all up and wiggled out from under
this making of it out what i was or became

or what i should or what I just shouldn't be

*for salsabil*

A plain of rigidity like grass
five inches high
                        gnarled and durable
            hard sitting place outcast left

to the eyes of god alone
with little more than strips

      of sunlight to crease the silence small
              breaths of dazzling dusk

or sunrise sit or stilt lifting cold
skin from our aloneness. Sit

          here not two handspans away
                  and listen
to a smoke
of my simple voice mark

            the urgency with stillness
    smell it with me water-like and thin.

I cannot save you or raise
your arms above

        the rising sludge but I promise
            to bend the blade press

each toe to the mud to you
and grip us until.

if I draw you again this
time years later it would

be on water clear paper
liquid the way it moves

your chest a target melted to
settle at the waist your

hair gray you gray you

*these portraits hanging on sheets*

they look like girl say if you look like girl
they look and girl say men men
they like to look and girl say the men look
like you and you is they girl men all those
walking hands girl say look if they like all those
girls if they look at those hands if girl walk if they
like look at girl all those men maybe you say look
like girl you say hands you walk if you if they
if you look you like girl if you walk like you like
girl if you look like them those girls that like
girls those men that like girls that like men
that like girls or like anything that pushed in
that walk with they do with they hands and they
say like like what they do when they do it when
you look like you like you like girl like you like
them and they hands they hands they walk
on you they hand you when and smush and stalk
when fight like you ain't girl or you are girl
or like you look like you a girl like you look like
them and them girl and they men only grasp
what they see what they feel what they
step on think like you girl no more than

and another one
        who is not deity nor queen no

fist no flower she does not
 have limbs

     nor does she rotate round her
    ball frame
                              she is not pearl held in

        the hand squeezed and released back on broken flint

   made firm and her
        skin does not peel off to reveal under

                the silver
     sap something liquid clean peach she is not

    beauty shimmering terminal guise not steel framed not

            lashes of copper not buttoned
       not brushed

     nor tresses of wire lean that I or
you or

he or they unbraid and baby she does not say

               just borrow my face or please

      (she cannot speak) *I just need you to love*
            me for she

this made thing written and crafted unbuild waits

                              for the sunset's long

          fingers of light to burn away the scars for
the end of well-meaning slurs

                    for the unneed of having to mask

                    and bake self into box gadget and rig it always the brown
                              clay in ware

            a monster seas through the twilight slosh to pluck
the small figures by their midriffs skywards

  to unlock a promise
of lightning cleansing a radiation rainblessed with all
that spit     tumbling
out dripping              salt     all gold             all steam

                  this monster's need so blind in the sound
                  track of the forgetfulness slumber the way windows should

stretch their             piercing         seams out
      to eat ocean
                              your voice
                  saying back your    words or mama's      in     your own way
each  syllable                                                       splashing
on the toasted wet rock the press

            of being known on the shoulder the legs bowed in     the small thunder
                              of standing

or      the      name    of                        water

when
the monster turns flesh colored and warm to ruckled *gogira* angry prehistoric bent thing

the breaking down of self for if a body
  is used too  wrongly or feared or left too long to rot unseen then it
                  might it      *ought it*        not it          too
            rise in the furor to  gather all
                              the parishioners  colleagues   from their fleeing
to open its mouth       dangle them      in front of its own     black twisting tongue

to      hem     and     stamp          and storm
and *say*     well at least    *think*
                   politely

        *you know it offends me that you still can't pronounce my name* what this man has placed on his skin ink

from the cage they kept him in
and swirl from the handles of a crockpot dogtags
whistling making you wish they were windows to his need
a thousand shards of horn each one built

of page bodyhair and wild the rage
and sighing of a good man gone green

unfathomable this attempt of comfort

the bicep sprawled on lawnchair as if this bodypiece could
bring cotton and gloss the air make full
the stale skywards make one a two riding east and
less bitter than the glide of salt kisses

dripping of minutes morewant then mustbe then sweep
and all the ways in which it is this a sort of shelf

legs loose waterisms that cover this man of one

good bright thing where pule and hollar fades
to bed his shuddering he is opening
there in the backseat or the ceiling stratosphere
one man speck then two then again one

                                                                                                                                                

      & being as they
     assume the woman
    part is underbelly doughy     fluid filled
    sacs of little  tiny mewling things  pappy
structure bound by echo you'd think


    that she'd sleep here  sheets with crumbs
     all her limbs stretched
     out to the doorway
 or else tucked under
        steel burka bars and of course shuddering

yet the lining of her
   silhouette peers
     over the tossed city like sunrise there are
spears here and twine
     in each of her fists
   and she is awake ready  to quake down
   on that body the silence
     before the throw


        I thought the boy inside would drive me
      gift me his shield chestwood curse word
    stratified between the folds
      hoard and army
     enough to make plates of this
       labor a wassail
       of servantless muster


   and she got down
  in the kitchen  like it wasn't nothing  mended our feet
     and showed him all up

                her name is what makes her bloom the afghani woman
                         her name staining her but slow almost aloud
      in morning in two rak'as where the forehead

  bruises the knee
             tastes the scars on the pale eyes to lace lazy
      manes of ascot rivers that brandish

      their silken toes round the ears
             and she must at least preen furious
her own beauty in the cool glare of men now only shadows and tiny stones thrown

      ever left to rot or rut their
own names into the three dots on the chin their bare
    feet sticking out of her pots of qorma

         so many browned bones
     for safe in her dressfolds callings
       of girls her sister or mother of her whispered and loud

     as the skin of pebble as the black
           goat hair or hard mats of reeds
                caresses only to remind her

       how she like weapon like birdhead
            pivoted watching her own
                   self kneel at the window how she
                         can turn and crown

   *queiro all y*
     *no bailes sola*
  with     your split
angling   and your silk
*vacila   azul*
    *la pista*
      *es aquí*
    the step is
slight    hanging
   *una sacudida*
     *olvidamos*
ourselves in this
sliding   this dance
    all   alone
   I need to
   remember
  *cada parte de ti*
  and your   movement
    *y tu  cuerpo*
  *su   presencia*
  is twirling like
*yo soy*   a bird
*en el aire*   flying
    *su*   shadow
reaching    *mano frio,*
  *acopio*   then bursting
     stones
    your beauty
   is   *tu ira*
*y yo soy*   with you,
   *canto   contigo*
   *mendigo dulce*
     waiting
*payaso   triste*
   soft   frowning

                picture
         gentle    *soldado*
   toy       *labios*
       laughing *a través*
             *de la ceniza*
            friend      boy
     *mi compañera de baile*
     *mi amante*
*no puedes*   hurt me
so let us     touch
       *de agua*     dance
   our faces    *besar*
     *nuestras lagrimas*
           honey   *queiro que*
   all of it    all of you *niño*
        all *a traves*
        like *algo de mi*

& sometimes I don't even like the little boy
those skinny arms and needy ways of

a sunken chest in a grown out fade

"I choke these fools" @10 years old and
desperate so desperate to stay over at my house a

little longer he falls asleep in the backseat as
I pass men at the metal doors grass too broke

to grow in all this blot plate of brick boxes the housing
authority deigned to maintain a kind

of service and corrective aid callous barbs
that beg thank you because hey it's not a bench

or a shelter or the laid down passenger
seat of a car and now his mother on the phone

spelling out e.v.i.c.t... just because
now with that other authority though she has two

children two part time jobs two crumbling left feet
back bent @31 where if I could I

would take her in my home
and this time sequester

her straighten her out with cool irons
and zumba and pottery or alvin ailey 'cause couldn't she dance

at one time @17 wasn't there butterflies and didn't
we bond those years ago over the ways

a body can stretch and move out away from everything
it's ever known but she says

no it is too late for that the three day notice already
came and there is no time left but to go back home

now time to go home now wake up now baby it's time
to go home and just try to sleep lay down

and sleep try anyway don't be sad
I promise to take you swimming again

next weekend.

*the law & how it makes us*

                    talk about rockets.
                I want to
            but not as an object so
                        bespoke or petal-dressed
        glared red with chains
                        passengers
    and hymns. nor silver flags
                        parapet like spades. people
                who can fly
                    unwoven in
            metal baskets
                        that free. get it and gather. these folks
                into grease
                    newly formed. 'cause one
                    makes up
                    freedom
        swimming or walking
                    unfurling wings
            with magnanimity.
                say this
                    we are leaving. say
                fuck America
                    the mothership is here. see this
                sword like
                    bursting through
                cloud
                    fold.
                    while we sit and taste this
            kinte-rimmed cup
                    bliss all
                    of it.
                us spent
                    fat
                    and full.  watching through space windows.

      the seat of
           this country's
    open purse.
trauma finally receding
         receding
      into
        ground.
    ash.
        and
        and.

*after Terrance Hayes, "Democracy is Dying"*

so wait… then there is only three
choices 3 choices to spell out the words
of governing or control or mastery
blood your knife with their flesh or
their push your it in between the skin

or bind it like feet to one and another goal kill…
fuck… why not converse like you do alone
pretending that Oprah wants to know
your particular answers to those

generic questions swimming in awkward
symposiums of silence or that bragging way

you read quotes aloud ahem… ahem – but two
sided not 1 and 2 and marry even with
that chain or pole or just… just the music as your

differing goals coalesce into some creamy
dominion but *yaass queen* without the conquest
america's gentle sister come home to dance and yes
that's a choice too fuck/marry/dance & dance dance

with me like you have tails to balance your naked
bowls atop your head – naked little feet – in dirt

unnamed and sticking out its belly to wait but
wait! for you can print to touchdown and grin to marry

and taste the one that loses = the lady unthinkable
undying diseased offstage too wise for
this consensus of free but unfree land of pink (unpink)

we just hide our deplorables under cabinets and i.
don't. think.  they can even understand me man the choice

so caught up bold lines we... just ain't the same
semantics brother that dear word –democracy– is alive and breathing
like oceans breathe outside all these

silly border wars (i hear you) all killing it marrying asking why
we. keep. fucking. the whole thing up

the little girl won
the lottery.
that's what they told her
over the phone.

that her name had been drawn and the coveted spot
in the good school
was hers if she could get there
on time and if she could work hard.

well that
was implied.

her mother was proud
telling all the relatives
　　uncle-to-be-avoided
　　grandmother in bed
　　young cousin too old
　　　　for chances
about how smart
the little girl was and how it was such
a good
thing.

that was
not implied.

the mother
never talked about the getting
to school.

the mother never mentioned the parts of the winning
that exist in the parts of the outside.

the little girl won
the lottery and the time
weeks
a few she'd
spend
if her mother
could get up that morning or
if the bus
was there or
if the little girl
wasn't too
tired or ashamed
to go
would be enough.

that is
implied.

because it has to be.
because it is what we all believe.
because I am making up this
story and telling
you the thing you already know.

a fiction
that is that
which might make you cry but doesn't really change
anything.

and

when they pulled her
name out of the bucket they didn't
look inside
her house

didn't track the roots like thin
tree rings
back to another
woman who found
something inside enough to fight
demons and taught in curse
and fire that same shit to her kin.

maybe that
woman just laid down not
on the bed but outside
herself from it and all and everything

              and isn't it
         This.

      this the same fiction
                you saw last night on television heroine raped
                in period drama
                slave women with perm.  no

             they pulled
                    a name from
                        a bucket and congratulated themselves
   on the good
   of what they were doing
   the chances they would give
   these poor
   poor black kids. and in the tale

they must be poor they must
be black
                they must be kids.

      this is lottery after all. there must be winners      and losers.

                      they
                            even
                            fought
                            over
                            who
            would
            get
                        to call all the winners
                        what poor administrative
                        soul who would be tasked with the
                        no.

as if
no
was not
in some way punishment.
the burden
of the victims to get the story straight.
the little
girl doesn't see the aftersmile.

the way
that pride deflates like a leaky jar.

                but then again.
                    there is no smile.
                        there is no pride.  there is no bucket.
            there is no jar.  no the little girl believes only
the moment
            a
            few
            weeks maybe
when all the world of possibility exists in her

                       brand new backpack and brand new school
dress. | explicit and new and clean.

We are struggling underwater. We are the sea. The water so cold. When they find us and pull us out our skin is ice. But in the water we feel warm. Our head bobs a few times. Upwards we and we can see sky, the blue water of the beach, the black bumps of the pier. It is like a magazine picture, bright wavy blue and we feel seaweed on our legs and we imagine that we see it in yellow and black. Down below is the water while fingers of black silk tickling us. and we feel the rush of opaque glass but silence. But there is nother down below When they pull us out our heart has stopped, our lungs full of water, but now drowning our heart beats like rattles or dull spoons. quiet down in the brown cloud. cause it is so afraid be are not we but drowning are We

& everything folds
the skirts ruffling waving through

the thighs the paper
letter bending as it falls the air

between us sound waves folding them
selves to connect your image to mine the touch

of one piece to the other be it by design
or suspended on an alchemist's pigments

and fever dreams drawn out in
mathematical lines that if you could explain this

would take 5 turns or three hundred
steps or you just pressing each end to the basic

shape the music that exists in the space beneath
the art form the medium of this

sound an orchestra like origami
or more but I am afraid of you

and it knowing that this recitation of some
paper's thin trail is the change

in the surface the making of the crease of new
memories and this time when again we

try to stack our flat bodies and our pairs
into groups love society rendering ourselves small

angry folded things that straight
figure of it only wants the return

of standing where you don't lose the thread like
last night your palms flat smoothing
the covers to find the folds here soft carvings

of pulp strokes contortions I cannot keep
waiting for you the want calligraphy

sung or compressed like a curl being
made all the lines rind and blend

/

splay hand open          wall and face the shoulders  or clavicle or splay finger brick
touch leg        eagle the crease of you

at elbow's inset
          at straining bleat then splay waist pivot paint
your skin is spread

your knee bent         your bleat

//

It was as if she danced jerking to the sounds of the block rain like excessive courses of old quilted towels stuffed in door jams heading against mother winter the smell of her punched to silt the cream of my hands the strength of my insistence and she was almost like a lover laid there arched over the wall by knuckles getting caught in fuzz and hair the smell of her or the other her that woman last week where this is a reasonable necessary routine search the statements that say otherwise that blame me should be ripped up and torn into sheets fluttering signs in front of the courthouse where it is no worry they give you a leave and they don't do anything so I shiver blue silver at the way it falls the fear that skewers the concrete blank brink walls where I detained each trespasser to stop or did I say go home go home and I want to go home and shut down and eat but I find myself screaming here so cold now the wet soup splashes to join the bruises on my wrists the aches in each line of bone my own break my own breaking like streetlamps those brick walls white then too quick to red to to red shower away

## III

When he        stops        me I        pause. I am polite. I        try to defuse. I        ask why. He        is        so _____.        I am        so afraid. He _____ me.

## IV

If we say they are _____ (insert name slur)?
If we say you don't Deserve? Need? Have a name?
If we convulse our ropes into our palms to unravel our ribs kangaroo neat?
If we breathe in tweets?
If we keep thinking that their breath is painted in hues as stark as the walls that make up our   streets while our while their bodies aren't bodies aren't glass petals that contain?
If we stop them and do not stop ourselves?
If we remake sex into weapons rape silent and unfilmable clean?
If we line them up by skirt and purse like bruised oranges underserving of the bowl
If we cannot control anything? If we say it wasn't a death? If we make it unspeak? If we hide it from our cameras? The shiver in the cold air, our spread of discontent like their bread is crumpling at our ankles, a climb to storm, a break? If we break? If we break them?

    Then

## V

That cop just felt me up. At least he didn't hit me.

## VI

You have your purse out itty bitty little strap on your wrist and your skirt tight around your

waist too late to change. There's brother, your best friend, sister, aunty right by your side in your mind, their hands up too or hip cocked 'cause this is a rite of passage the stop and wall. You will be fine

little sister though be calm because it might turn and flounder this unlullaby into something broken a neck a contract an understanding of engines a whine up momentum that drives this day to the rest of days after this day. And you

stare at the wall his exhale on your neck his paunchy face like the color of air of all those standards that sit watching you from every screen though you know invisibility is both a curse and a friend. Where you think

is his hands. The hand that holds the stick the stick that can hit and you remember the purse when it is over when he has sent you home to sit in your own driveway to shake your legs pressed together the purse like a band-aid still dug into your wrist thin fake leather a

new part of your skin but here your purse here heavy and real as the warmth of the wall real as the sun baked against your palm real as his hands down there searching as if something that was lost that day

could ever be found again.

## VII

And when it is over if it ever is over if it ever is if

& yet again she stirs and this time you must acknowledge the occupation
in the breathe the smell of musky hair like a woman unwashed

has just sat down her thigh pressed to your own damp seat
suturing you to her so that her warmth spills from your mouth

while her scars shine like branches that creep up her neck shiver
around her a robe clacking with your shoulder blades you are

occupied you are being dragged forward by the clasp link sunk
in your neck by the language you both speak so that even this prelude

rips the curtain and makes the stage before it start a box of fire flayed
meat and flesh ripe with conquest the knives sprinkled like leaves

and thrush burning pale oil silhouette shade to a page her chest now
hungry red eating the ribs to gasp its way across her body your body to

make tilt the chin of this happening again and again the
burning cage and you midway between always remembering even as

the scene shifts to a sink and a bowl a smell of char that asked you to
uncover your palms and dare the fire to finger each feature as if you could

reach in to break each rib and erase the knowledge of how it hurt
the making of those when first arrived and you were stopped &
                                stop
                    I say stop
                                    'cause here I stop

for if the hand moves the arm must follow the shoulder the neck
the knee back to embers gorging cartilage red metal body typic

and honey and she is not real what has happened to you is not this foe right now
you are burning two letters in the sink and just outside the window

a tree's spinelike branch watches the saplings meeting their beryl
sky the picture an opposite of rage and rerememberings but if these letters

these artifacts of being taken or used burn then she must to burn you
might soon be free one day to wander in the unoccupied sky so blue its

dances the soot from the air and the smell of her hair waiting for any small
trigger spark to  tickle caress seek

fight to be this ugly
           scrunch up to
     be this puckered
            with what should
        be smooth
       hate that
       which runs clear        scrap with the skirt
                                the legs hooded
                   thighs all ceiled          wild
                  bag dress stuffed
          as ridiculous as
          hoodie with sewn in brims        maybe just trying
                                     to beat the cracks snippets
                 of iron lines strolling
           lazy treads that instead
       should hike up pleated
         denim and just you
know flow just like
      camouflage blackwashed
   burkaed and        so what that I would       so rather be
                                                ugly twirl the naked
                                       ballerina stretch her

                              show off her panties boxers
                    or lack thereof legs
               like the pillars of a
                  chantry fierce
                 as forked motes driven down
          into the ground into the chest
                    strutting like peacocks and queens
         down each avenue

& if it were under my arm i may even then not fight but step grin fetch the collar and pretend that i can handle it this ghetto

mentality the great state and stamp and dictation filling my words like law with acceptable pastiche so that

this scream at my ancestors for not digging me out of this nest has no true translation how can i stop wearing the orange jumpsuit for the way

it blinds aid and county where even us woke and laid back on the wet wood still squint our eyes into a horizon that has to goddamn be so goddamn far away

'cause ain't no real romance in this kind of poverty just a chained dance where hands on necks insists that pain feels good and us saying yes yes for our one more gust of air to fill our chests as

it fills the hollow of the trunk pushing out the smell of piss in the barbed room we survived y'all those old ones croak their mouths of callous scabs lips breaking to say to us

    that the way back means – that the answer is – that we survived because –

    spine and driftwood and bargain and hidden wings like spurs *i was born poor*
                                               patience
        *I can be free*
        prancing

      *i refuse to not see the beauty in it all* our bellies
        sacrifice

      our
      straining and yes baby yes smiling through for what
        *we know we are*

& you made too out of that bark bone heavy tired bend body mouth eye into *joy all hard found & neat*

or on tv the astrophysicist says that if we pack too much into one space time thing is space like a star? instant of a place we may create a black hole but I think of data like the scratchings on a table or the entries of the thin encyclopedia or the flapping CD the thumbed drive even how we make our body need with emotional density all while I see all that data stuff as if it were a pancake pressed and flattened to be petted on its head a gentled coddled kind of fiend limbs just itching to grope remember and perhaps grieve so here I change the channel finally because stone tablet or CD or drive is only an emptiness that that sifting astrophysicist flirting just a bit I think with the chair of the physics department never talked about and I want the meat of it well the taste anyway the spice the singing how it feels my daughter's hair coiled into my fingers with my mama's voice brass a snare in the background of each of my memories or this even the writing of it the flat page and raised typeset rushing always to condense its secrets outward and weren't you astrophysicist lady only supposed to be explaining gravity how it holds and makes us connect each thing to the other to the next for truly I turned to you because I only wanted to teach my daughter something simple we can watch something else baby not her grandma hardly able to rise from the bed too heavy and pressed with pain to grasp onto me comb my hair bend me backwards all around her and how much I wanted that layer of her hands pressing my scalp where I can just shrink down to forget the explanations of why always why I always hold on so tightly to the hard stuff why I fall so fast full of what has happened or better what is happening how it swaps position greedy because that lady smiling at that man is right it is inevitable this little girl's life in my own full of my mother's own and the thick of it is only to be collected like fingerbones or muscle maybe stacked layered like soup and

or that is not mean or that
is
mean I want to say to the ambiguously phrased sigh and turn away the mouth melte
at the
corners the quick cup of each eye the screams in my head always in my head at yo
wrong your
words
wrong your
shoulders wrong
your longing for
the placement of perfect palm or even pink hair coiled caressing top of fat nose
wrong and spanish
like croutons salty logged wrong in the jaw but waiting thick 'cause I don't look
the part to say *yo soy bonita*
too black
and too
closed and that is I say even cruel but underneath almost kind a cement bolting the breat
back to the eye
lash exposed
bent backwards like the spine suspends itself and screams dripping skin you canno
say this in
this crowd
you cannot
like metal
or pierce your tongue with skullbones that have afros and be country and educate
you cannot say I
don't
understand or I am more always I am more than this that what you can see because thi
is mean to
be known
mean to not
be inside we must keep the room breathing be at ease even when your neck bones
gyrate politeness and

your feet
scrunch
back into a
small ball of weft as you know you all of us just be learning not to feel and
learning not to need and I need it
really
need it you
know I need
it you
need it baby
the nod the I see you my sister the I know your joy and pain and it ain't
wrong 'cause I
know you know it too

might even like it when she does this make me like babies in tissue paper pink pale yellow streamers pinned up and groomed or even shake my jaw into rattler toys the smell of her thick as grown things     that collapse into the colored sand of heritage as fragileas this push for what is ground what is cardboard what is solid to be folded and  punched square into good for. At one time I did not want to be here stuffed     into bowls touching myself on the chin     waiting plucking stray hairs and crust from the corners     of each lid as if awakeness could change the hollow sounds of her not talking and     not touching me back for when you are small smaller     an ungrown thing you know but cannot ask for     hum hug gentler wrapped swaddled thumping bone under skin. Can I sit on your lap?     Or sleep in your bed or     with you be with you so the dark hulking in the small bent spaces of the corners of the room your own body & her     mind gentle just a bit. So you like it might like it just might when she quiets and turns she's getting older inward again gone to     what for her was so bright and     blinding it couldn't had happened was had ever been.

& so we miss it the
first day the
first
day of not
many
days and we
miss the narratives
the beginnings
of it the
calling of the
names the
names of
us renamed into
offensive entities
like those obscene
drawings like
those cartoons black
faces sketched
around white
mouths or those
words they mean
when say this
is what
hysterical is
so we miss
our head
into the
taste of
it the bit the
sound of a
heavy hand on
the ECT machine we
miss the
curtain going
up the rustle of

the theater the
gathering of
the crowd
that looks
like clouds pacing
themselves into
pots of marsh
mallow jiggly with
anticipation so
many reporters
with so many
pieces of
paper wrapped in
so many pens
to capture
every word
that condemns
always
those damn
questions
*how could you*
*your*
*why what were*
*when* – yeah we
missed it
      we stopped at the door to
pause and collect
                each dandelion
        petal shriveled
but still spinning
like a helicopter silent
      as that first
           morning
each collected then
      lined up

      glided carefully back
    on the stalks
to trace the bony
    stem down into the dirt
to find the
radicle
the tuber
each
branched
out
then
counted
blessed one
by one the
vein thin
but so
proud
settling far
under
the porch a
fiberlike
ore or
quilt
    that task that took hours
decades and we missed
    your show but when  I think back to that time all  I remember is
      that I couldn't remember
        where I was supposed to be
          that I had gotten lost in the
        smell of the earth
       far from sundials
         watches
         good fights
         that push
         to make right

                my hand holding
        something
                        that looks suspiciously
                                    like a spade

*sing: drinking muddy water*

black woman be the mule of the earth she been drinking muddy water but she know what she worth black woman be the mule of the earth she been drinking muddy water but she know what she worth black woman be the mule of the earth she been drinking muddy water but she know what she worth black woman be the mule of the earth she been drinking muddy water but she know what she worth black woman be the mule of the earth she been drinking muddy water but she know what she worth black woman be the mule of the earth she been drinking muddy water but she know what she worth black woman be the mule of the earth she been drinking muddy water but she know what she worth black woman be the mule of the earth she been drinking muddy water but she know what she worth black woman be the mule of the earth she been drinking muddy water but she know what she worth black woman be the mule of the earth she been drinking muddy water the mule of the earth she been drinking muddy water but she know what she worth black woman be the mule of the earth she been drinking muddy water but she know what she worth black woman be the mule of the earth she been drinking muddy water but she know what  she worth black woman be the mule of the earth she been drinking muddy water

                                  **black woman**    black woman    **black woman**
black woman    black woman    black woman    black woman    black woman
                **black woman**    black woman    black woman
        black woman    just out here thirsting with her crayon
**black woman**    her score all giddy enough to
black woman    dance on north sides rain like forest pine
green shouting pale steal aways but grabbin'
it always by the waist a dance in the dank shack
with flat
granite feet she be answering phones little screens
screaming her name octave dropped bass while pant greets
each ping with smile for if
even she wanders she can always lick
the envelope wheeled white witch
ride in her chariot of crème gold like the shape of a star
was etched on the boulevard for
her saying black woman baby girl you just out here
swimming like crawl doing the thang

        be the mule be the mule be the mule this to make
     dirt the dreg of her coils muscle **be the mule**
   **be the mule** that switch to shore to break

**be the mule** be the mule dirt green vines a lash baked
      into the batter butter on each hustle be the mule
   be the mule of this to make

be the mule **be the mule** it be hard we know this fake
     winding of man and toil to justle be the mule
        **be the mule** that switch to shore to break

**be the mule** be the mule it bend the back of her to take
    crown gone in the fat inevitable rustle be the mule
     be the mule of this to make

the earth she the earth she
the earth she weeping maybe but I think she laughing
the earth saying each fool that press the chest she
the earth she
the earth she ain't fast enough to slip the bite and since
the earth she she don't have teeth well then it must
the earth she
the earth she be a private juggling a memory to poke
the earth she and rib that keeps her out of the shit
the earth she
the earth she in her diaper the earth coughing up
the earth she plastic or plastick we love to blowing shit
the earth she
the earth she up even if she be curled old but baby
the earth she small and does it matter that we used
the earth she
the earth she that we used that we used her up took
the earth she her toil to our own beds to fluff shuffle
the earth she
the earth. she our shoulders like there would be always
the earth she this rusty room to come back to like
the earth she
the earth she the plate done cracked 'cause it do that is
the earth she earth crack open and pass on sweet soft as gum

    been   drinking
been drinking         been drinking
          been      drinking

    too       long  and now

   my belly is   swole and as   big as the    mountain

so it takes everything that is every

       character every role all the piece of all bodies of
               muddy      water

      it into its own lips to   compress them  an ideal of

        muddy water       muddy water
                           you
              muddy     water
               your   choosing

but she know it and you know it and he know it and she
over there must at least suspect **but she know**
something is up because how
you come out of bed how come you peeking naked
feet out covers up like there be
tiny slippers decorated with leaves but she know
how come ain't no phone
in your hand begging you for touch 3 big & red unread pings that
be saying **but she know** you most certainly
ain't going to be enough and don't you remember how bad
it always bruises purple lines but she know
that spread blade thin up the arms to the neck the forehead
the sajda mark a bloom of moss and brush roots showing through **but she know**
why you damn happy girl don't you remember
these chairs don't fit your body that bed and weighted cover
is just a gurney where the water be lapping the wood a river so
soft-rotted wide even if you but she know
swam even if flying mermen the whale something
would beg for bags of shells to catch you & **but she know**
you ain't never not had your
own face this face and this forest ain't never not your own
I see you but she know in that red coat covering the zigged scars
like out there like there's a clearing asking you to dance asking you
to dance **but she know**
asking you
to rule

what she worth is this: bird
or bullet balanced maybe the hollow point a slug that pierces a plump body waving its footprints in moss or gray earth like the sky warm just barely touches skin

## what she worth

what she worth is this: fish
see that thing swimming there popcorn thin colored balls of glide where river water too is as blue as the sunlit pathway and where to go is a small taste of salt on tongue

## what she worth

what she worth is this: things to do
always the womaneverything eating sugar always more shore and children leading youth to the promise of landing on edge of joy we say freedom but well

## what she worth

what she worth is this: fight
banners and names in the pocket aching feet the swell of a chant that becomes a kind of remedy for at least it cradles the rage and makes the laserbeam riot and plume

what she worth

what she worth is this: time
'cause cure picked up its skirts to run away last night and all that is left to do is prick the muscle with a stylus made of weak bark spongy like a song you sing alone in the car

what she worth

## what she worth is this: what she worth
all and nothing and all and more and she black woman be the mud of the earth, water in her mouth all this carpet and dirt at her feet caressing each mule toe delicate like drinking her up

        & so we are in the ribs of it the goddess while she knits

        sweaters licks lips
        of clouds as
        the pearl of fingernails
        those

        white gristle bars draped
        with lilac-like stone
        coils of shell I'd raise
        up from my

        knees stamp into dust
        inked on the insets
        of the ankle snares
        in each foot a

        stretched hide drum now (hear
        it?) the film to
        the pound that
        gathers this room a

        whole mess of
        the want in this
        world hung on
        the wall twirling like

        gnats to be one
        cord of connection
        battering &
rumbling making bend the stamp of the ichor of one wall

        back down to
        floor (for

I'd want to
feel
It) from

the inside from
inside of
me the way it
starts now marrow

music & you never
daring to leave your
dancing without
breath without needing

to sing the sounds we
make raw
(now again ever) bodylike
fluid that

rhymes the slip of
it 'cause it hurts (don't
it child) revving up shivering it
hurts it repeats

it strums trying
to (always this
trying to) heal be

more unhurt get up fly sip go wing drown stand touch click open
clip patch hand scratch find start stir

&(and)

# About the Author

Nikia Chaney is the author of *us mouth* (University of Hell Press, 2018) and two chapbooks, *Sis Fuss* (2012, Orange Monkey Publishing) and *ladies, please* (2012, Dancing Girl Press). She has served as Inlandia Literary Laureate (2016-2018), and her poetry has been published in *Sugarhouse Review*, *491*, *Iowa Review*, *Saranac*, *Vinyl*, and *Pearl*, *Welter*. Her memoir, *ladybug*, is out from Inlandia in 2022.

# About the Artist

Janine Aberg holds a BA in Performing Arts from the University of the Nations, and an MA in Conflict Transformation from Eastern Mennonite University, Center for Justice and Peacebuilding. She has won prizes at fine art competitions on the Hawaiian Islands, worked for a summer with Philadelphia Mural Arts, and exhibited with a group of fellow artists at the Olympic games in the UK 2012. Her art is strongly influenced by color, light, and by her love for dance, movement, and animals, expressing the wealth of beauty and feeling that is born out of the confluence of suffering and the joy of life. She is deeply influenced by her country of origin (South Africa), living in Hawaii, and travelling around the world, and loves to experiment with the intersectionality between fine art, dance, theater, music, and healing. Her art hangs in many countries including the USA, South Africa, China, Germany, Sweden, and England.

## About The Word Works

Since its founding in 1974, The Word Works has steadily published volumes of contemporary poetry and presented public programs. Its imprints include The Washington Prize, The Tenth Gate Prize, The Hilary Tham Capital Collection, and International Editions.

Monthly, The Word Works offers free literary programs in its Café Muse and Poets vs. the Pandemic series. Word Works programs have included "In the Shadow of the Capitol," a symposium and archival project on the African American intellectual community in segregated Washington, D.C.; the Gunston Arts Center Poetry Series; the Poet Editor panel discussions at The Writer's Center; Master Class work-shops; and writing retreats in Tuscany, Italy.

As a 501(c)3 organization, The Word Works has received awards from the National Endowment for the Arts, the National Endowment for the Humanities, the D.C. Commission on the Arts & Humanities, the Witter Bynner Foundation, Poets & Writers, The Writer's Center, Bell Atlantic, the David G. Taft Foundation, and others, including many generous private patrons.

An archive of artistic and administrative materials in the Washington Writing Archive is housed in the George Washington University Gelman Library. The Word Works is a member of the Community of Literary Magazines and Presses and its books are distributed by Small Press Distribution.

wordworksbooks.org

# The Hilary Tham Capital Collection

Nathalie Anderson, *Stain*
Mel Belin, *Flesh That Was Chrysalis*
Carrie Bennett, *The Land Is a Painted Thing*
Tara Betts, *Refuse to Disappear*
Doris Brody, *Judging the Distance*
Sarah Browning, *Whiskey in the Garden of Eden*
Grace Cavalieri, *Pinecrest Rest Haven*
Nikia Chaney, *to stir &*
Cheryl Clarke, *By My Precise Haircut*
Christopher Conlon, *Gilbert and Garbo in Love*
    &   *Mary Falls: Requiem for Mrs. Surratt*
Donna Denizé, *Broken Like Job*
W. Perry Epes, *Nothing Happened*
David Eye, *Seed*
Bernadette Geyer, *The Scabbard of Her Throat*
Elizabeth Gross, *this body / that lightning show*
Barbara G. S. Hagerty, *Twinzilla*
Lisa Hase-Jackson, *Flint & Fire*
James Hopkins, *Eight Pale Women*
Donald Illich, *Chance Bodies*
Brandon Johnson, *Love's Skin*
Thomas March, *Aftermath*
Marilyn McCabe, *Perpetual Motion*
Judith McCombs, *The Habit of Fire*
James McEwen, *Snake Country*
Miles David Moore, *The Bears of Paris*
    &   *Rollercoaster*
Kathi Morrison-Taylor, *By the Nest*
Tera Vale Ragan, *Reading the Ground*
Michael Shaffner, *The Good Opinion of Squirrels*
David Allen Sullivan, *Black Butterflies over Baghdad*
Maria Terrone, *The Bodies We Were Loaned*
Hilary Tham, *Bad Names for Women*
    &   *Counting*

Barbara Ungar, *Charlotte Brontë, You Ruined My Life*
        &   *Immortal Medusa*
Jonathan Vaile, *Blue Cowboy*
Rosemary Winslow, *Green Bodies*
Kathleen Winter, *Transformer*
Michele Wolf, *Immersion*
Joe Zealberg, *Covalence*

CPSIA information can be obtained
at www.ICGtesting.com
Printed in the USA
JSHW031254160223
37717JS00003B/24